Common Core Lessons & Activities: Native Americans

By Carole Marsh
Published by Gallopade International, Inc.

Printed in the U.S.A. (Peachtree City, Georgia)

TABLE OF CONTENTS

G: Includes Graphic Organizer
GO: Graphic Organizer is also available 8½"
download at www.gallopade.com/clien
(numbers above correspond to the graphic orga

Early Native Americans

Read the text and answer the questions.

The first people to live in North America are known as Native Americans. The first of these people are thought to have crossed over an ice bridge between Asia and North America – migrating into North America at Alaska – nearly 20,000 years ago.

Based on charred bones and arrowheads found at ancient sites, archeologists believe the first Native Americans were big-game hunters who hunted herds of large mammals. Because of their food source, archeologists also believe most early Native Americans lived a nomadic lifestyle, having no permanent home and traveling from one place to another in search of food.

As the Ice Age ended, and much of the ice melted, many large mammals died out. As the environment changed, the early Native American's subsistence, or methods of obtaining food, changed as well. Native Americans began to forage (hunt and gather) small animals and plants to eat.

Native Americans continued to move through North America, and 10,000 -15,000 years ago, they began to raise plants for food in what is now central Mexico. From there, agriculture spread to many areas of North America. This subsistence method, known as agriculture, changed the way Native American people lived. Agriculture allowed people to settle in one location and form communities. As they worked together, they developed new ideas and skills. As more and more people settled in one place, complex societies like the Mayan, Aztec, and Mississippian cultures formed.

1. Define nomadic and subsistence as they are used in the text.
2. List and define three subsistence methods used by Native Americans.
3. Match the following questions to whether they are best answered by paragraph 1, 2, 3, or 4 of the text. Then answer the questions.
   A. _____Why did Native Americans become hunter-gatherers?
   B. _____Where did the first Native Americans come from?
   C. _____How did agriculture impact people in North America?
   D. _____How did the subsistence method of the first Native Americans affect their lifestyle?

Mississippian Culture

Read the text and answer the questions.

Long before Europeans arrived in North America, Native Americans settled the land. The tribes that settled along the Mississippi River were known as the Mississippian culture. These tribes shared characteristics and ways of living.

The Mississippian culture is best known as "mound builders" because of the large earthen mounds scientists have found at the remains of villages. Some mounds were rounded on top, but most were flat-topped like a platform. On top of these earthen mounds, the Mississippians built houses, temples, and public buildings.

Nearly all Mississippian tribes grew corn (maize) as their main crop. Large-scale farming allowed the Mississippian tribes to settle in one place, improve craft skills, and develop complex societies.

In Mississippian societies, one or several "chiefs" often held power, and the highest and most important members of society usually lived atop the highest mounds. The Mississippian culture shared resources. Tribes created a vast network of trade spanning from the Atlantic Ocean to as far as the Rocky Mountains.

1. Why are the separate tribes that settled along the Mississippi River considered part of the group known as the Mississippian culture?
2. A. What is the main idea of the text?
   B. Create a main idea graphic organizer and show how the main idea is developed and supported with details in the text.
3. List three effects of agriculture on the Mississippian culture.
4. Which dictionary entry best describes a branch of science most likely to study Mississippian "mounds"? Explain why.

Geologist *— a person who studies Earth's natural physical features and events such as how the earth was formed, earthquakes, and volcanoes*
Archeologist *— a person who studies human history and culture through the recovery and investigation of artifacts and other physical remains*
Paleontologist *— a person who studies forms of life existing in prehistoric or geologic times through the recovery and examination of fossils*

Regions of North America

Read the text and answer the questions.

Native American tribes occupied all regions of North America. Because different regions have different climates and resources, the tribes in each region developed different ways of obtaining food and built different types of dwellings.

In the forests of the Northeast, tribes such as the Iroquois and Algonquin fished the rivers and lakes using canoes. They hunted large wildlife for food and to make warm fur clothing. They sometimes raised crops for food. From tree branches and bark, they built "longhouses" and "wigwams" (made by pulling young trees together into a rounded structure) to protect themselves from the harsh winter weather.

In the warm Southeast, tribes such as the Cherokee, Chickasaw, and Seminole built "chickees" – small huts of mud, grass, and river cane. Their warm climate allowed Southeast tribes to stay in one place and farm – corn, squash, and beans were popular crops. They also hunted and fished.

Tribes of the Great Plains, such as the Arapahoe and Comanche, hunted the buffalo – an important source of food, clothing, and weapons. Most lived a <u>nomadic</u> lifestyle, meaning they constantly moved from place to place. Since Plains tribes followed the migrations of buffalo across the Great Plains, they lived in triangular-shaped tents known as "tepees" which could be easily taken apart and carried long distances.

Plateau tribes, such as the Nez Perce, moved from place to place as seasons changed. They often built a permanent winter village and seasonal spring and summer villages. They often built "wigwams" and "longhouses" with the floor dug several feet into the ground and the roofs covered with mats they made from tule grass. Plateau tribes fished, hunted small animals, and gathered edible roots, berries, and vegetables.

In the dry Southwest, tribes such as the Pueblo, built "pueblos" – houses several stories high made of clay bricks dried in the hot desert sun. Southwestern tribes also grew crops like corn, squash, and beans.

California tribes included the Kayasha Pomo in southern California, who hunted the waterfowl in nearby marshlands using slingshots and nets, and the Yurok and Hupa in northern California, who fished salmon in the mountain streams and gathered acorns in the forest. Many California tribes cut wood from the cedar forests to build "plankhouses" that looked similar to simple European shacks.

Northwest tribes, such as the Kwakuitl and Haida, formed permanent salmon-fishing and hunting communities. In the northernmost areas, the Inuit hunted seals and built "igloos" from the ice.

1. Use the text to complete the chart by identifying each Native American dwelling pictured and the region(s) where it was found.

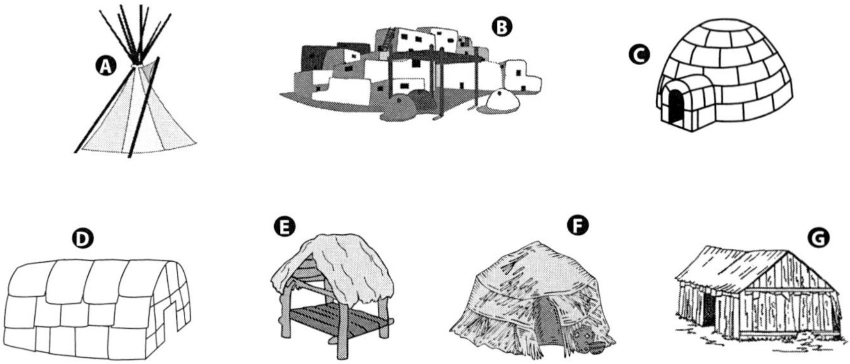

Picture:	What it's called:	Region(s) where it was common:
A		
B		
C		
D		
E		
F		
G		

A. Use the text to define <u>nomadic</u>.
   B. Why were many Native American tribes nomadic?
   C. List three tribes that were nomadic.
   D. How did a nomadic lifestyle affect Native Americans' housing?

2. Writing Prompt: "How was a tribe's way of life affected by its region?"
   A. Write a short essay to answer this question. Include at least three ways a tribes' way of life was affected by its region. Include examples from the text to support the effects you describe in your essay.
   B. Edit your essay. Your writing style should be somewhat formal. Be sure to include linking words and transitions between ideas. Proof your essay for accuracy.
   C. Create a multimedia presentation based on your essay.

Columbian Exchange

Read the text and table to answer the questions.

The Columbian Exchange is the widespread exchange of plants, animals, culture, diseases, and ideas between the Eastern Hemisphere (Old World) and Western Hemisphere (New World) during the time of European exploration and colonization of the Western Hemisphere. The Columbian Exchange is significant because so many of the things introduced from one part of the world to another had monumental and lasting effects on the future of the world. The Columbian Exchange also marks a turning point in Native American history.

1. Answer A-D based on the text above:
   A. What is the Columbian Exchange?
   B. When did the Columbian Exchange begin?
   C. Who did the Columbian Exchange affect?
   D. Why was the Columbian Exchange important?
2. For each cause below, list a direct effect and an indirect effect.
   A. Europeans inadvertently bring diseases to the New World.
   B. Europeans bring horses to the New World.
   C Europeans introduce domesticated livestock to the New World.
   D. Native Americans introduce Europeans to new crops.
3. Describe a cultural idea that Europeans brought to the New World. Explain how it was positive and how it was negative.
4. Explain why European contact with the New World is described as a "turning point" in Native American history.
5. List three different groups of people that benefited from the Columbian Exchange and for each group, describe one way they benefited.
6. List three different groups of people that suffered from the Columbian Exchange and for each group, describe one way they suffered.
7. Describe and give at least two examples of how the Columbian Exchange impacted:
   A. population
   B. migration

Item	Direction	Why	Effect	Effect	Effect
Horse	OW to NW	It was a faster transportation method	Made conquest of Native Americans easier for Europeans	Provided Native Americans a more effective way to hunt buffalo	Horse became domesticated and was used for farming
Livestock including pigs, cattle, and chickens	OW to NW	These were domesticated animals (not wild)	Animals overgrazed and destroyed many crops and groundcover	Farming became more efficient and dependency on farming increased across America	Huge cattle ranches and cattle drives increased the westward movement of people
Potatoes & Corn	NW to OW	These crops are inexpensive to grow, and they are nutritious	Helped feed growing population in Europe; became important crops for population growth	Dependency on potato crop caused famine when potato crop failed; caused many Irish to migrate	Became a staple of diets worldwide; fed many people and allowed people to live longer
Sugar	OW to NW	It tastes good	Became a part of diets everywhere	Europeans forced Native Americans to work on sugar plantations	Europeans brought many Africans to be slaves after Native American population decreased
Disease	OW to NW	Native Americans had no immunity to diseases like smallpox	Killed nearly 95% of all Native Americans	European settlers were able to take Native American lands more easily	Africans were brought to New World as slaves
Concept of land ownership	OW to NW	Native Americans did not view land as "owned" – Europeans did	Europeans settled on Native American lands	Native Americans did not grasp the concept of land ownership until much of their land was gone	Native Americans were forced to relocate from their homes to reservations
Gold	NW to OW	European explorers were expected to find gold and send it to their countries	European explorers enslaved many Native Americans and forced them to mine for gold	Many Native Americans died from the harsh conditions inflicted by the Europeans	European countries had more money to spend on goods from other countries

Clashing Cultures

Read the quotations and answer the questions.

The building of our little fort...has been a good work. Had it not been for the recent killing of young Alexander Askew... the friendship of the Indians might not have been suspected, and this very necessary work might have been postponed... I have no confidence in the friendship of these savages, and have always felt that we have been warming a viper which will some day show us its fangs. Our only safety, in my opinion depends wholly upon...the preparation we make in our defense.

—Francis Cample, European colonist, in Pennsylvania 1740

We hear on all sides that this Governor and the Bostonians say that the Abenakis are bad people. 'Tis in vain that we are accused with having a bad heart. It is you, brother, that always attack us. Your mouth is of sugar but your heart of gall. In truth, the moment you begin [speaking] we are on our guard.

Brothers, we tell you that we seek not war. We ask nothing better than to be quiet, and it depends, brothers, only on you English to have peace with us...We acknowledge no other boundaries of yours than your settlements whereon you have built, and we will not... [let] you pass beyond them. The lands we possess have been given us by the Master of Life...

—Atiwaneto, Abenaki leader, in French Canada 1752

1. A. Describe Cample's opinion of Native Americans.
   B. Cite evidence from the text to support your response.
2. A. Describe Atiwaneto's opinion of European settlers.
   B. Cite evidence from the text to support your response.
3. How did "the recent killing of young Alexander Askew" affect:
   A. Cample's opinion of the Native Americans?
   B. The actions of the Pennsylvania settlers?
4. A. Who is the intended audience of Atiwaneto's speech?
5. Gall has a bitter taste. How does Atiwaneto's sentence, "Your mouth is of sugar but your heart of gall" characterize the English?

Native American Leaders

Read the text and answer the questions.

Chief Powhatan was a leader of the Powhatan Indians of Virginia. Powhatan and his daughter Pocahontas developed a friendly relationship with the first Jamestown colonists. After Chief Powhatan's death, the Powhatan Indians fought against colonists settling on their land. After several years of conflict, the Powhatan Indians were all but destroyed by fighting and disease.

Pontiac led a rebellion of Native American tribes against British and colonial traders in the Ohio region in 1763. Pontiac's Rebellion contributed to the British Proclamation Act of 1763.

Sequoyah developed the Cherokee alphabet to give his people the ability to communicate on paper. The U.S. viewed the Cherokee people as more civilized because of their alphabet. The Cherokee government was able to write its own constitution.

Tecumseh was a Shawnee chief who opposed treaties that sold Native American land to the U.S. government. He called for Indian nations to join together to oppose white settlement. He led many small Indian nations in Tecumseh's War, and later joined the British in the War of 1812. He was killed in battle in 1813.

Chief John Ross, leader of the Cherokee nation, tried to prevent Cherokee lands from being taken by U.S. settlers. The continued increase in the number of settlers and the discovery of gold on Cherokee lands made his struggle difficult. Ross argued, debated, gave speeches, appealed to Congress, and signed treaties, but he ultimately failed to save Indian lands. In 1838, the U.S. forced the Cherokee westward to Oklahoma on the Trail of Tears.

1. List a direct effect of each of the following events:
   A. Ongoing conflict between Powhatan Indians and colonists
   B. Pontiac's Rebellion
   C. Sequoyah's invention of an alphabet
   D. Treaties that sold Native American land to the U.S. government
   E. Discovery of gold on Cherokee land
2. Describe at least one similarity and one difference between Tecumseh and Chief John Ross.
3. **True** or **false**: Native Americans were united against the U.S.

Thoughts on Land

Read the quotations and answer the questions.

A) "[They] never cared for land or dear or bear. When we Indians kill meat, we eat it all up. When we dig roots, we make little holes. When we build houses, we make little holes. When we burn grass for grasshoppers [for food], we don't ruin things. We shake down acorns and pine nuts. We don't chop down the trees. We only use dead wood. But the white people plow up the ground, pull up the trees, kill everything. The tree says, "Don't. I am sore. Don't hurt me." But they chop it down and cut it up. The spirit of the land hates them... They blast rocks and scatter them on the earth. The rock says, "Don't! You are hurting me." But the white people pay no attention."

B) "What good man would prefer a country covered with forests and ranged by a few thousand savages to our extensive Republic studded with cities, towns, and prosperous farms embellished with all the improvements which art can devise or industry execute, occupied by more than 12,000,000 happy people and filled with all the blessings of liberty, civilization, and religion?"

1. What is the common theme shared by the two quotations?
2. Summarize the point of view expressed in each quotation.
3. What strategy does each speaker use to promote his point of view? Provide examples.
4. Identify at least two examples of personification in the first quotation.

Analyze each statement and identify whether it best supports the point of view of **Text A** or **Text B.**

5. ____________"Gaining farmland is essential to a growing nation."
6. ____________"All good things come from land, to be shared equally."
7. ____________"Industry will change the wild into a great civilization!"
8. ____________"The spirits of all things are disturbed by American settlers who use the land for selfish purposes."

READING INFORMATIONAL TEXT

Indian Removal

Read the text and answer the questions.

In 1783, the Treaty of Paris gave land west of the Appalachian Mountains, including much of the Iroquois, Shawnee, Choctaw, Cherokee, and Creek tribal lands, to the United States. Within the United States, each Native American tribe was a <u>sovereign</u> nation. Each "nation" was free to own land, elect leaders, make laws, and make lawful agreements, called treaties, with the U.S. government.

Originally, Native Americans negotiated land with the U.S. government in what became known as the "treaty system." However, land treaties between the U.S. and Native Americans were often ignored or overlooked by white settlers who intruded and settled upon Native American land. The discovery of gold on Cherokee lands in Georgia added further desire for the land owned by the Native Americans. In the 1820s, many states asked the U.S. government to put an end to the settlers' "Indian problem."

In 1830, President Andrew Jackson signed the Indian Removal Act. This act allowed Congress to remove Eastern tribes from their homes to a land reservation west of the Mississippi River. From 1831 to 1847, the U.S. government forced most of the eastern Native American tribes to march west to land in Oklahoma. Many Native Americans died on the long journey, which became known as the Trail of Tears.

1. For each event, list a direct effect:
   A. The Treaty of Paris of 1783 is signed.
   B. Gold is discovered on Cherokee land in Georgia.
   C. Andrew Jackson signs the Indian Removal Act.

2. Which of the dictionary entries for <u>sovereign</u> in the box best matches the use of the word in the text? Explain.

noun	***A supreme ruler, especially a monarch***
adjective	***Fully independent and determining its own affairs***

3. Why did settlers ignore Native American land treaties?

4. What name is given to the relocation of Native Americans from the Southeast to reservation lands in Oklahoma? Why?

Native American Culture

Choose one Native American tribe to research. Use at least two online resources to answer all the research questions and complete the graphic organizer. Draw a picture or paste an image to represent each topic. Then follow the instructions for writing and presentation.

Southeast	*Northeast*	*Great Lakes*	*Great Plains*
Cherokee	Powhatan	Shawnee	Sioux
Seminole	Algonquin	Huron	Blackfeet
Chickasaw	Iroquois	Miami	Cheyenne
Choctaw	Pequot	Oneida	Comanche
Creek	Wampanoag	Ottowa	Arapaho
			Dakota

Northwest	*Pacific Northwest*	*Southwest*
Pomo	Chinook	Navajo
Ute	Nez Perce	Apache
		Pueblo
		Hopi
		Mojave

Research Questions

LOCATION: Where did they live? (region; type of housing)
FOOD: What did they eat? How did they get their food?
CULTURE: What cultural rituals were important to them?
ART: What artwork did this tribe make?
INTERACTION: How did the tribe interact with U.S. settlers? Did any tribe member(s) have significant impact on U.S. history? Describe.

Writing & Presentation

1. Organize your research into an informative visual such as a poster or digital slideshow. Write accompanying text to explain the culture of your Native American tribe.
2. Give your presentation to your class.

After everyone gives their presentation, discuss Native American culture as a class and answer these questions:

A. Identify common themes and similarities between tribes.
B. Describe major differences between the tribes.
C. How did Native Americans impact the history of the U.S.?
D. How were Native Americans impacted by the history of the U.S.?

LOCATION

FOOD

CULTURE

ART

INTERACTION

Westward Expansion

Look at the table and maps to answer the questions.

Westward Expansion Event	Years
Trail of Tears	1838-1839
California Gold Rush	1849-1858
Transcontinental Railroad	1863
Indian Wars	1865-1890

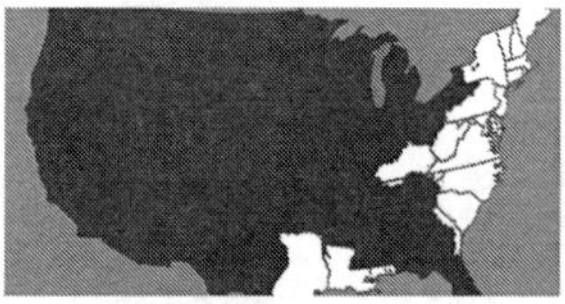

A. 1784

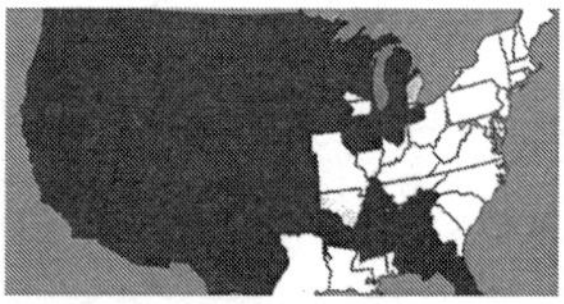

B. 1810

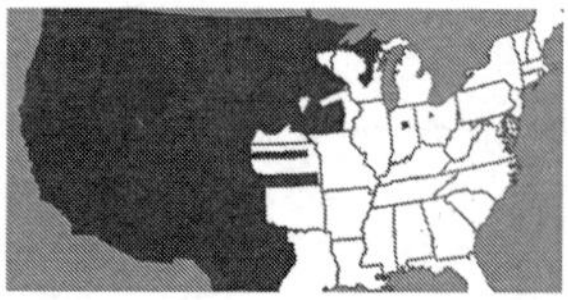

C. 1840

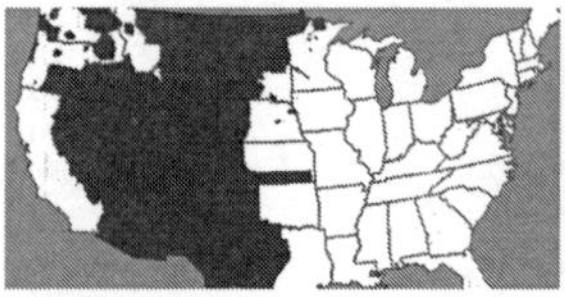

D. 1860

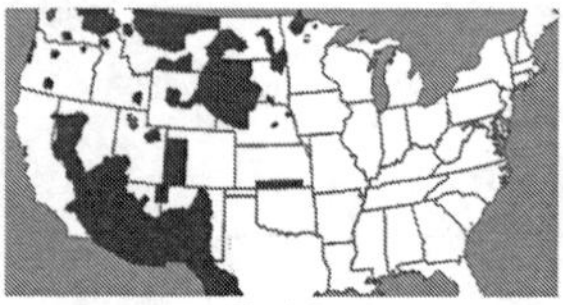

E. 1870

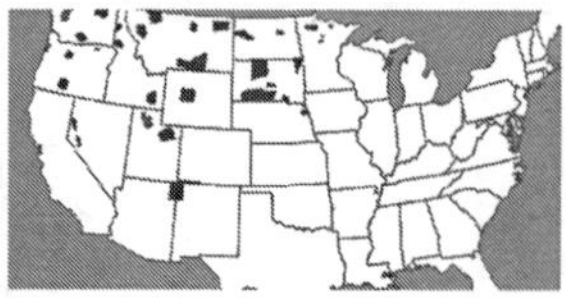

F. 1890

Dark areas = Native American Land   *White areas = United States land*

1. Write a descriptive title for the series of six maps.
2. Which map best shows the direct effects of the Trail of Tears?
3. Which map best shows the direct effects of the California Gold Rush?
4. Which map best shows the direct effects of the Transcontinental Railroad?
5. Which map best shows the direct effects of the Indian Wars?
6. A. Make inferences to explain why the 19th century in American history is described as the time of "westward expansion."
   B. From who's perspective is this title appropriate?
   C. Write a similar title to appropriately describe the 19th century in American history from the perspective of Native Americans.
7. Write a paragraph to explain the relationship between "westward expansion" and Native American history. Cite details from both the table and the maps to support your explanation.

Plains Indians & the Buffalo

Read the text and answer the questions.

> Without [the buffalo] we were nothing. Our tepees were made of his skin. His hide was our bed, our blanket, our winter coat. It was our drum, throbbing through the night, alive, holy. Out of his skin we made our water bags. His flesh strengthened us, became flesh of our flesh. Not the smallest part of it was wasted. His stomach, a red-hot stone dropped into it, became our soup kettle. His horns were our spoons [and bowls], the bones our knives, our women's awls and needles. Out of his sinews we made our bowstrings and thread. His ribs were fashioned into sleds for our children, his hoofs became rattles... The name of the greatest of all Sioux was Sitting Bull. When you killed off the buffalo you also killed the Indian—the real, natural, "wild" Indian.
>
> John Fire, Lakota Sioux Indian

1. A. What is the main idea of the text?
   B. What method does the author use to support the main idea?

2. Complete the infographic by describing how the Plains Indians used each part of the buffalo.

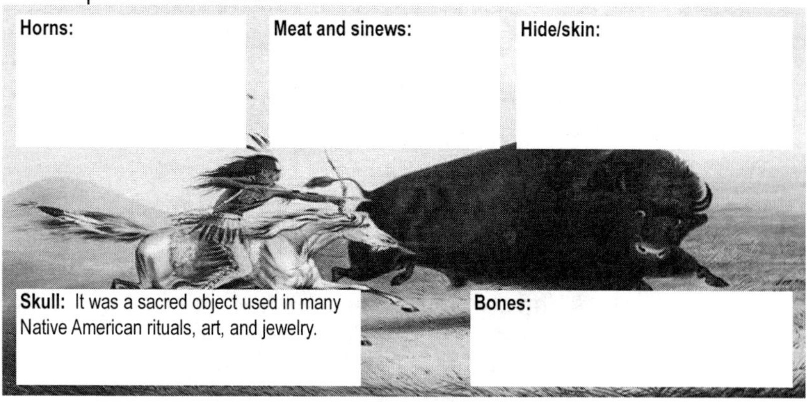

3. American settlers did not see a need to protect the buffalo. They killed thousands of buffalo to sell their hide and horns. In 1800, there were 65,000 buffalo. By 1890, only 1,000 buffalo remained.
   A. Compare and contrast the importance of the buffalo to American settlers with the importance of the buffalo to the Plains Indians.
   B. Predict how the decline in buffalo population would affect the Plains Indians' ways of life. Cite evidence from the text to support your prediction.

Indian Wars in the West

Read the text and answer the questions.

Massacre at Sand Creek In 1864, members of the Cheyenne and Arapaho settled on the Sand Creek Indian Reserve in Colorado. They had peacefully negotiated the land treaty with the U.S. government. Without orders, a militia troop commanded by U.S. Colonel Chivington attacked and killed over 150 unprepared Native Americans at Sand Creek, including women and children.

Fetterman Massacre The Bozeman Trail led American settlers directly through Sioux hunting grounds in southern Montana. Red Cloud asked the U.S. to close the Bozeman Trail but was ignored. In December 1866, the Sioux warrior Crazy Horse led 200 warriors in an attack on Colonel William J. Fetterman and his men who were camped along the Bozeman Trail. The Sioux warriors killed over 80 soldiers. The U.S. government closed the Bozeman Trail.

Flight of the Nez Perce When gold was discovered on Nez Perce land in 1863, American settlers flooded into Montana and Idaho and the U.S. government took back 6 million acres of land promised to the Nez Perce. Chief Joseph, leader of the Nez Perce, refused to remove his tribe from the land. Around 2,000 U.S. troops were sent to remove the Nez Perce in 1877. Chief Joseph led 700 Nez Perce in four long battles against the U.S. Chief Joseph eventually surrendered and moved to the smaller reservation.

The Battle of Little Bighorn Sitting Bull was a strong Sioux leader who believed that white men should leave Sioux territory. He refused to sign several treaties, and continued to lead his tribe on traditional hunting grounds in Montana. When gold was discovered in 1872 in the Black Hills, American settlers flocked to Sioux, Cheyenne, and Arapaho lands and U.S. General Custer and his troops were appointed to force Indian tribes to move onto smaller reservations. In 1875, the Sioux formed an alliance with several tribes. In June 1876, Sitting Bull had a vision of soldiers falling from their horses. He predicted the arrival of General Custer, and called on the allied tribes to come help prepare a defense. On June 25, General Custer and his troops attacked the huge Indian village. On June 26, Crazy Horse, Chief Gall, Sitting Bull, and many other warriors surrounded General Custer and his troops at the Little Bighorn River. Using spears and rifles, the Native Americans killed General Custer and all of his soldiers within an hour.

Red River Wars From 1868 to 1874, Cheyenne and Kiowa tribes fought against encroaching American settlers by raiding homes and settlement wagons. The U.S. army responded in 1874 by moving friendly tribes onto smaller reservations and attacking all others. The U.S. military crushed Indian resistance by hanging Indian warriors, killing their ponies, and capturing women and children.

The Battle of Wounded Knee By 1889, the Sioux were pushed onto small reservations with few sources of food. An Indian prophet told the Sioux of the Ghost Dance, a ritual that could restore lost land to the Indians. The Ghost Dance spread to over 25,000 Sioux. U.S. military leaders suspected a revolt and attempted to arrest Sitting Bull. Sitting Bull resisted and was killed. Then, in December, 1890, the U.S. military rounded up 350 starving Sioux and took them to a camp near Wounded Knee Creek. The Sioux were told to give up any weapons. A shot was fired and the U.S. soldiers responded by killing over 300 unarmed Native Americans. This battle marked the last major Native American resistance in the West.

1. Use the text to describe at least two attempts at peaceful negotiations between the U.S. and Native Americans.
2. A. Identify three acts of violence by Native Americans.
   B. Identify three acts of violence by the U.S.
3. Give three reasons why peaceful negotiations gave way to violence.
4. Describe the role of prophecy and visions in Native American culture. Cite evidence from the text to support your response.
5. Identify a cause and effect relationship from each section of the text.

Cause:	→	Effect:
Cause:	→	Effect:
Cause:	→	Effect:
Cause:	→	Effect:
Cause:	→	Effect:
Cause:	→	Effect:

Assimilation

Read the text and answer the questions.

After the Indian Wars, the United States developed a new solution to the so-called "Indian problem." Instead of continuing to battle Indian tribes across the West, the United States supported assimilation, a plan to force Native Americans to give up their culture and become part of white American culture.

The process of "Americanizing" the Native Americans started with the Dawes Act. This act divided the vast Native American lands into smaller reservations. It also gave small plots of land to Native Americans to own as property. Native Americans who owned land were "given" U.S. citizenship. By making Native Americans U.S. citizens, the government took away tribes' rights to self-government. Additionally, as U.S. citizens, Native Americans were subject to U.S. laws.

Under U.S. law, Native American children were forced to attend "federal boarding schools for Indians." U.S. soldiers gathered Native American children from the Indian reservations and took them to boarding schools far away from their family and tribal leaders. At boarding schools, Native American children were taught American history and American culture from the U.S. point of view. Native American children were forced to speak English, learn American values, wear American clothing, and practice American industrial skills such as carpentry for boys and housecleaning for girls. Separated from their parents, children did not learn much Native American culture. They were not taught their tribe's oral history, dance, art, and other ways of life. One Native American child recalls: "I remember coming home and my grandma asked me to talk to her in our native language and I said, 'Grandma, I don't know how.'"

1. A. Define assimilation as it is used in the text.
   B. Who wanted to assimilate the Native Americans? Why?
2. List five direct effects of the Dawes Act.
3. List five ways federal boarding schools attempted to assimilate Native Americans.

4. Use the text and make inferences to complete the graphic organizer from the perspective of the U.S. government.

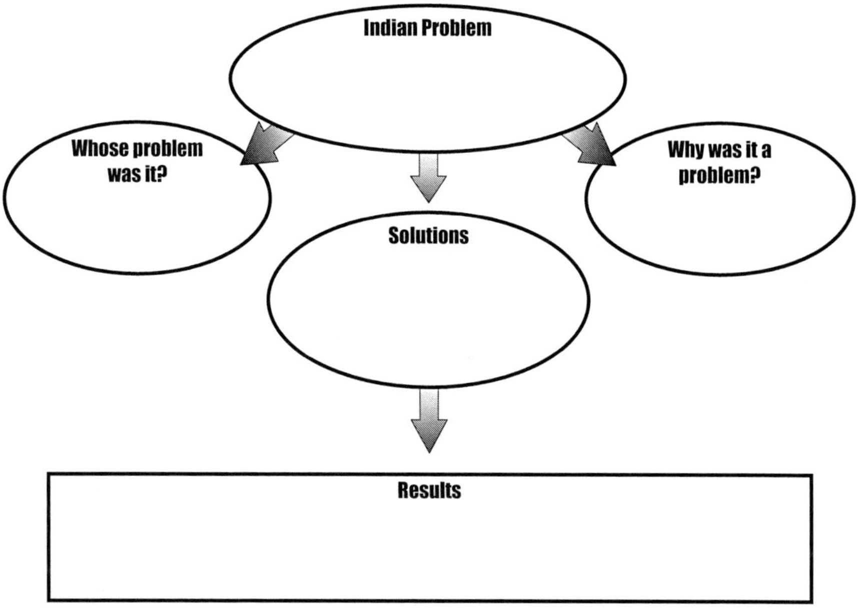

5. Read the quotation and answer the questions below.

> "A great general has said that the only good Indian is a dead one... In a sense, I agree with the sentiment. But only in this: that all the Indian there is in this race should be dead. Kill the Indian in him, and save the man." Colonel Richard Pratt — Superintendent of a federal boarding school

A. Summarize Colonel Pratt's point of view about Native Americans.

B. Which sentence from the quotation best summarizes the purpose of the federal boarding schools?

6. Look at the two photographs – both are of the same person, a Native American before and after attending a federal boarding school.

A. Compare and contrast the physical appearance of the Native American in the two photographs.

B. Label the photographs "before assimilation" and "after assimilation".

7. Write a short essay about the "transformation, inside and out" of Native Americans at federal boarding schools. Cite evidence from the text, quotation, and photographs. Proofread and edit your work.

PRIMARY SOURCE ANALYSIS

General Allotment Act

Look at the poster and answer the questions.

INDIAN LAND FOR SALE

GET A HOME OF YOUR OWN

EASY PAYMENTS

PERFECT TITLE

POSSESSION WITHIN THIRTY DAYS

FINE LANDS IN THE WEST

IRRIGATED IRRIGABLE

GRAZING

AGRICULTURAL DRY FARMING

IN 1910 THE DEPARTMENT OF THE INTERIOR SOLD UNDER SEALED BIDS ALLOTTED INDIAN LAND AS FOLLOWS:

Location.	Acres.	Average Price per Acre.	Location.	Acres.	Average Price per Acre.
Colorado	5,211.21	$7.27	Oklahoma	34,664.00	$19.14
Idaho	17,013.00	24.85	Oregon	1,020.00	15.43
Kansas	1,684.50	33.45	South Dakota	120,445.00	16.53
Montana	11,034.00	9.86	Washington	4,879.00	41.37
Nebraska	5,641.00	36.65	Wisconsin	1,069.00	17.00
North Dakota	22,610.70	9.93	Wyoming	865.00	20.64

FOR THE YEAR 1911 IT IS ESTIMATED THAT **350,000** ACRES WILL BE OFFERED FOR SALE

For information as to the character of the land write for booklet, "INDIAN LANDS FOR SALE," to the Superintendent U. S. Indian School at any one of the following places:

Courtesy of Library of Congress

1. A. What is the purpose of this poster?
   B. What can you conclude about the time period of this poster?
2. Make at least 3 inferences about the land for sale in this poster.
3. What does this poster indicate about the future for Native Americans?
4. What does this poster indicate about the future for American settlers?
5. Write a response to this poster from the perspective of a Native American or an American settler. Read your response aloud to your class. Can your audience accurately determine your point of view?

PRIMARY SOURCE ANALYSIS

Navajo Code Talkers

Read the text and look at the entry from the Navajo code talker's dictionary. Then answer the questions.

In World War II, the U.S. needed to be able to send military orders and information in a way that the message was clear to the person it was intended for, but unreadable by anyone else. At first, messages were "coded" by machines. However, machine-coded messages could be easily decoded. The consequences of U.S. strategy being known in advance could cost thousands of lives, and possibly the outcome of the war. A better way to communicate was needed...and found. Between 1942 and 1945, over 400 Navajo Indians acted as "code talkers" for the U.S. Marines. They used their Navajo language to send coded messages. The Navajo could send and decode messages more quickly than any machine. And, the German and Japanese never cracked the code!

MEANING	NAVAJO PRONUNCIATION	LITERAL TRANSLATION
ALASKA	BEH-HGA	WITH WINTER
AMERICA	NE-HE-MAH	OUR MOTHER
BOMBER PLANE	JAY-SHO	BUZZARD
BOMB	A-YE-SH	EGGS
GERMANY	BESH-BE-CHA-HE	IRON HAT
PLATOON	HAS-CLISH-NIH	MUD
FIGHTER PLANE	DA-HE-TIH-HI	HUMMING BIRD
MINUTE	AH-KHAY-EL-KIT-YAZZIE	LITTLE HOUR
PROBLEM	NA-NISH-TSOH	BIG JOB
ROUTE	GAH-BIH-TKEEN	RABBIT TRAIL
SPAIN	DEBA-DE-NIH	SHEEP PAIN
TANK DESTROYER	CHAY-DA-GAHI-NAIL-TSAIDI	TORTOISE KILLER

1. A. Describe the role of Native Americans in World War II.
   B. Why were Native Americans uniquely able to do the job they did?
2. Make inferences and write 3 journal entries as a Navajo Code Talker. Include entries from your first day, two weeks later, and three months later. Describe where you are, what you are doing, and why.

PRIMARY SOURCE ANALYSIS

Recalling the Past

Read the text and answer the questions.

> "In the old days, before the white people came up here, there was a boat sailing on the ocean from the south. Because before that [the Kashaya Pomo] had never seen a boat, they said, 'Our world must be coming to an end. Couldn't we do something? This big bird floating on the ocean is from somewhere, probably up high...' they promised Our Father [a feast], saying that destruction was upon them. When they had done so, they watched the ship sail north and disappear... They were saying that nothing happened to them—the big bird had sailed northward without doing anything—because of the promise of a feast... Consequently they held a feast and a big dance."
>
> *– an oral story shared by the Kashaya Indians; excerpt from Kashaya Texts*

PART A: Use the text to determine who or what is being described.

1. "the old days"
2. "the white people"
3. "this big bird floating on the ocean"
4. "Our Father"

PART B: Make inferences from the text to answer the questions.

3. Write a title to express the main idea of this text.
4. What can you infer about the author of this text?
5. A. What was the Kashaya Pomo people's reaction to the boat?
   B. Why did the Kashaya Pomo people react in this way?
6. Which word best classifies the excerpt above? Cite evidence from the excerpt to support your answer.
   A. first-hand account B. historical memory C. factual report
7. Foreshadowing is a literary device by which a later event is predicted or indicated beforehand.
   A. In what way does this text accurately foreshadow the future?
   B. Cite evidence from the excerpt that Native Americans believed in the concept of foreshadowing in real life.

Cultural Vocabulary

Use a dictionary and other resources to complete the graphic organizer for each vocabulary word.

- chief
- colonization
- confederation
- culture
- moccasins
- nation
- nomad
- powwow
- reservation
- tepee
- treaty
- tribe
- westward expansion

DEFINITION

FACTS/CHARACTERISTICS

WORD

HOW IT RELATES TO NATIVE AMERICANS

Correlations to Common Core State Standards

For your convenience, correlations are listed page-by-page, and for the entire book!

This book is correlated to the Common Core State Standards for English Language Arts grades 3-8, and to Common Core State Standards for Literacy in History, Science, & Technological Subjects grades 6-8.

Correlations are highlighted in gray.

PAGE #	READING *Includes:* RI: Reading Informational Text RH: Reading History/Social Studies	WRITING *Includes:* W: Writing WHST: Writing History/Social Studies, Science, & Technical Subjects	LANGUAGE *Includes:* L: Language LF: Language Foundational Skills	SPEAKING & LISTENING *Includes:* SL: Speaking & Listening
2	RI RH . **1** **2** **3** **4** **5** 6 7 **8** 9 **10**	W WHST . 1 **2** 3 **4** 5 6 7 8 **9** **10**	L LF . 1 2 3 **4** 5 **6**	SL . 1 2 3 4 5 6
3	RI RH . **1** **2** **3** **4** **5** 6 **7** **8** **9** **10**	W WHST . 1 **2** 3 **4** 5 6 7 **8** **9** **10**	L LF . 1 2 3 **4** 5 **6**	SL . 1 2 3 4 5 6
4-5	RI RH . **1** **2** **3** **4** **5** 6 **7** **8** 9 **10**	W WHST . **1** **2** 3 **4** **5** **6** **7** **8** **9** **10**	L LF . 1 **2** **3** **4** 5 **6**	SL . 1 2 3 **4** **5** 6
6-7	RI RH . **1** 2 **3** 4 **5** 6 **7** **8** **9** **10**	W WHST . 1 **2** 3 **4** 5 6 7 8 **9** **10**	L LF . 1 2 **3** **4** **5** **6**	SL . 1 2 3 4 5 6
8	RI RH . **1** **2** **3** 4 **5** **6** 7 **8** **9** **10**	W WHST . 1 **2** 3 **4** 5 6 7 8 **9** **10**	L LF . 1 2 3 **4** **5** **6**	SL . 1 2 3 4 5 6
9	RI RH . **1** 2 **3** 4 **5** 6 7 **8** 9 **10**	W WHST . 1 **2** 3 4 5 6 7 8 9 10	L LF . 1 2 3 4 5 6	SL . 1 2 3 4 5 6
10	RI RH . **1** **2** **3** **4** **5** **6** 7 **8** **9** **10**	W WHST . **1** **2** 3 **4** 5 6 7 8 **9** **10**	L LF . 1 2 **3** **4** **5** 6	SL . 1 2 3 4 5 6
11	RI RH . **1** **2** **3** **4** **5** 6 7 **8** **9** **10**	W WHST . 1 **2** 3 **4** 5 6 7 **8** **9** **10**	L LF . 1 2 3 **4** 5 **6**	SL . 1 2 3 4 5 6
12-13	RI RH . 1 2 3 4 **5** 6 **7** 8 **9** **10**	W WHST . 1 **2** **3** **4** **5** **6** **7** **8** **9** **10**	L LF . 1 **2** **3** **4** 5 **6**	SL . **1** **2** 3 **4** **5** **6**
14	RI RH . **1** **2** **3** **4** **5** 6 **7** 8 **9** **10**	W WHST . **1** **2** 3 **4** **5** 6 7 **8** **9** **10**	L LF . 1 2 **3** **4** **5** **6**	SL . 1 2 3 4 5 6
15	RI RH . **1** **2** **3** 4 **5** 6 **7** **8** 9 **10**	W WHST . 1 **2** 3 **4** 5 6 7 **8** **9** **10**	L LF . 1 2 3 **4** **5** **6**	SL . 1 2 3 4 5 6
16-17	RI RH . **1** 2 **3** 4 **5** 6 **7** **8** 9 **10**	W WHST . 1 **2** 3 **4** 5 6 7 8 **9** **10**	L LF . 1 2 3 4 5 6	SL . 1 2 3 4 5 6
18-19	RI RH . **1** **2** **3** **4** **5** **6** **7** **8** **9** **10**	W WHST . **1** **2** 3 **4** **5** 6 **7** 8 **9** **10**	L LF . 1 **2** **3** **4** **5** **6**	SL . 1 2 3 4 5 6
20	RI RH . **1** **2** **3** 4 **5** 6 **7** **8** 9 **10**	W WHST . **1** **2** 3 4 5 6 7 **8** **9** **10**	L LF . 1 2 **3** **4** 5 6	SL . 1 **2** 3 **4** 5 6
21	RI RH . **1** 2 **3** 4 5 6 7 **8** **9** **10**	W WHST . 1 **2** **3** **4** **5** 6 7 8 **9** **10**	L LF . 1 **2** **3** **4** 5 **6**	SL . 1 2 3 4 5 6
22	RI RH . **1** **2** **3** **4** **5** 6 7 **8** 9 **10**	W WHST . 1 **2** 3 **4** 5 6 7 8 9 **10**	L LF . 1 2 3 **4** **5** **6**	SL . 1 2 3 4 5 6
23	RI RH . 1 2 3 **4** 5 6 **7** 8 9 10	W WHST . 1 2 3 4 5 6 7 8 9 10	L LF . 1 2 3 **4** 5 **6**	SL . 1 2 3 4 5 6
COMPLETE BOOK	RI RH . **1** **2** **3** **4** **5** **6** **7** **8** **9** **10**	W WHST . **1** **2** **3** **4** **5** **6** **7** **8** **9** **10**	L LF . 1 **2** **3** **4** **5** **6**	SL . **1** **2** 3 **4** **5** **6**

For the complete Common Core standard identifier, combine your grade + "." + letter code above + "." + number code above.

In addition to the correlations indicated here, the activities may be adapted or expanded to align to additional standards and to meet the diverse needs of your unique students!